*Grocery List Poems*

by Rhiannon McGavin

Not a Cult

Los Angeles, CA

For information, contact books@notacult.media.

ISBN: 978-1-945649-31-8

Edited by Sam Sax
Proofread by Daniel Lisi
Cover Design by Cassidy Trier
Editorial design by Julianna Sy

Not a Cult
Los Angeles, CA

# contents

# Grocery List Poems

Rhiannon McGavin

## Pith

You want to be naked in the water
                but if you did what you wanted, you'd cry half the time.

All morning you shelled pomegranates
        for a kind new year, the membranes collecting
                in a crescent on the kitchen table    the skins
mottled thick like old bandages kept on out of superstition.
There's a trick to it    though you just clawed
        at the fruit that hungry way, shred by shred.

        Now you don't know what to do
with your hands,    standing on the beach    while a mirage of holiday clothes
trembles down the shore. On sand everyone slips like a child
                learning to walk, even rabbis. They're wading out
to their ankles, the husbands
    with their pants rolled up,    the grandmothers lifting their skirts    above the water,
        the teenagers half-somber, casting away their current sins
to the ocean in breadcrumbs    torn rose petals    tender enough to fit a mouth
        the tide folding over their little hurts.

You're staring at the horizon like it's the dull edge of a blade
        rather than a house key. Your coat pockets
                flicker with grocery lists and receipts, the gap
    between your desire and ability. Yesterday
            you couldn't find any scrap paper and wrote *eggs* on your left wrist.
Lately you've been sounding out some facts to see if it's still impossible—

                I was torn into my body. There was
                nowhere safe to count the days.
                Time unlatched from my limbs so
                I left. A callus grew to protect
                the red hours. But the kid who
                screams at the bottom of my head
                has started panting. Soon I'll ask
                what she wants to drink.

Empty
        heels, empty    loafers on the yellow sand
                            around you, the socks wilting
                    from their husks.
                                    You're coming into the moment
            how you undress before a new lover.   There's always a part
    where you have to close your eyes,    open to the soft dark
                passing over. You don't remember yet
        but at the most gone you prayed for the joys
                of every peach fuzz baby on the bus and whoever was holding them
            through the turns. Even then
        you would choose to take your shoes off
                and step through the grass walking home to feel
    the warm dirt beneath the tickling green.

Look, you're barefoot.
The sand under your heels
is the sand under your heels.
There's dead bees here, unburied in the footprints,
and you know they can still sting, still curled
around their own needle, who can blame them,
half their body a weapon, a defense.          Nobody's coming to apologize.

You're downhill running      past the sins gathered on the shoreline
like eyelashes crushed with tears, and the sea's kissing the white hem
of your dress and you're pushing through the water, blood-warm,
the pulse of a wave growing and then you feel   the wave,
the ripples of your own wake          the hourglass of your body set right,
and those people you love on the beach          don't understand why
you're out so far but it's enough that they can see you,      you're part
of that blue spiral,      your feet leaving      the ocean floor, a champagne brine
lifted in a waltz,          the linen dress soaked to your skin
and floating, legs free, the water carrying
you carrying yourself
up where every breath is new as the late sun sprays off you
like juice burst from pomegranate seeds between your teeth,
your head thrown back, your nails raw
in the salt after tearing away the pith

# Writing a grocery shopping list before going to the market is a poem to me.

## —Agnès Varda, *interview*

# Manifesto in an unknown language

No, I couldn't sleep, I'm building my loves
from the smell of rain and the bus driver's
soft wave when I'm broke, from a sea that carves
cracked bottles into gems, and a stranger's
laugh runs a vein of silver through the night,
a love cut from the dark when a kissing
scene fades on a film screen. Say the last time
someone touched me with a tender feeling
and I'll eat the clock. Name the next time, win
all the lucky pennies I've thrown away
waiting for that love like a nasturtium,
the petals with their birthday candle flame,
hot and sweet. The kind of love in my steps
where empty rooms are only rooms you've left.

# Top note

There must be a tree rooted to the dusty floor of this
          yellow evening bus for all that it smells of pear blossoms, the crushed

white flowers spread on the workday air although now
          I see you beyond our fellow dozing travelers here, you

by a window with your dark hair twisted
          up, leaving the back of your neck smooth above your blue collar

and surely there, you spritzed the perfume
          before going wherever you're going, the fog tendriled

back to me, swaying on the silver pole, my mouth
          a touch open as it was when I walked with the other little girl

unsupervised to the old orchard for green pears
          like birthday money and uncut jade, green pears so full

you had to commit to each bite, a promise, both hands
          needed to swell the curve picked from the sun side of a tree

which caught the most sugar, fruit warm
          as the July bursting around it and then another,

of course, how she would pick each pear with a twist, delicate
          as how she dropped a white mouse in the aquarium of her garden snake

before we came here to these trees, grown past
          their corset grid, the roots tangled and hidden as this day, pulp-drunk,

pear juice over our faces like a second skin when we
          jump into the spring where we could have drowned but didn't,

water deep and clear as a crystal ball and rippling
          our legs into harmonica songs, and still the tang

of pears in your mouth like a gulp of wine
          stolen from the dinner table and the blooms

thick on the breeze as you step
          off the bus now, and I'll never know if your name

bends the sunlight, honey, we'll never touch
          but over your pulse you take with you this sweetness.

*And well, quite independently, the next day, you came
into the café through that little swinging door,*          says
Aragon called Louis to Elsa Triolet called Ella and she does,
finding her young lady steps like walking through tide pools
in the Coupole Bar as they in their 70s recreate
the moment they met decades ago for Varda's public
broadcast documentary, which runs about 20 minutes,
short as breakfast. Ella pauses with her bare right hand
to steady the door. Her swing coat's a calla lily around her,
one holy button in the middle, 3/4 sleeves, and a brooch
of what looks like a horse mid-gallop through the black
& white grain over her heart. Then the film skips and
the camera pulls in a bit tighter as she walks through
the door again, the same dark velvet glove on her left hand,
the same silk scarf tucked over her silver hair
in place of the fur hat they remember her wearing that first
day, those eyes of Ella like wind chimes across the screen.
Behind her the café is an aquarium of empty chairs.
When Louis holds her baby picture and recounts the tiny
girl in a straw bonnet memorizing her dialogue
for a Chekhov play, it feels as though someone had been
there in the half-dark bedroom while she stumbled
through the words for an invisible crowd, someone who
shared the loneliness and magic. Once more the movie
cuts back, closer, and Ella walks bold through the door,
and how many versions of that strut did Varda collect
for this 3-second clip? Stretching their glance to make
sure you felt it? All that old flammable film,
the undeveloped histories on the studio floor, the x-ray
figures gathered to stitch 1928 from 1965, and 40 years is
a long time anywhere, baby. Picture it in their dailiness,
Ella on the street outside, Louis playing dice against
himself just before the lightning. Before the friends filled
their home with portraits of the couple, their faces so
familiar to the other that they could see a few lines
of pencil and know instantly, instantly. And here on this
little stage, after the blacklists and prisons and papers,

after they stayed revolution's sour children. After the evenings when the famous novelist sets the table while the famous poet rinses a head of romaine lettuce, enamored by the spring green, seagrass green leaves with violet crests, the leaves which begin ruffled and loose then grow crisp and small the more he washes, the spiral's beauty crafted by the space between, until he's holding a pearl of lettuce, which is a poem not because it can be explained, but because it was torn by hand, with care, and lifted soft to her teeth. Before she's buried in the garden they made, Ella walks offscreen to join Louis at the bar, the camera follows, their faces lined as the tangled stems of a strawberry patch. Later the young director asks if the poetry made her feel loved. The key light sings a high note from Ella's eyes, one brow arches. *Oh no! They aren't what makes me feel loved. Not the poetry. It's the rest.*

## Crush

Not that, but the firstest love
in the old neighborhood that you would cross
to walk the dog in front of her house,
just in case. The whole way there
your heart would shiver like a box of matches
as you rushed through the concrete churn
of your city with the poodle mix
in conspiracy to strut down the street
whose name you never learned, knowing it
by feel alone, your neck screwed
to keep the other girl's house always in sight:
what must be her bike
sprawled in the driveway, red curtains
closed with light spilling out or else open
to a hallway where she must
drum her bare feet down to deeper rooms
where she'd sit on the kitchen counter
with her girl-legs dangling or practice scales
on the caramel cello she wheeled around school,
her fingers tough from the strings. Never mind
what you'd do if she actually
saw you: catch fire and die, probably.
You loved: the bony knob,
a green peach, on the back of her neck,
the sugar-gap in her front teeth, the handful
of inches she had on you, each a little star
to wish on in the constellation you told
of this girl, the subject of dandelion-blown prayers
and lucky coins, every word she said to you
polished into a song. Up one sidewalk,
down the other, and the whole way back
with nothing new to worship but next time,
next time. Of course, her house
was really on the next street over
which struck you long after
you stopped watching the loquat tree
where she didn't live bloom & rain.

When someone does touch you
finally you leave the hot room
with splinters between your hips.
The late bus home glances past it,
your best house, the blessed sidewalks
pearly under streetlights,
open as the first curve
in a seashell where the living thing
had carved spirals with its living
and then gone. You remember
being told it was the whole ocean
rushing in the conch when it was
only your own pulse echoed
but you still hold it up,
hear your blood sing.

# Canoodle

AK — will you marry me?
XO PS   J+G   C+F   A+I
MP <3 EG scratched white

into the bamboo like chalk
for hopscotch in the Makeout Corner
of the Botanical Garden,

by the artificial stream
with actual snapping turtles.
I'm on a bench worn down

by so much teenage wriggling,
a borrowed sweater of green stalks
tall around me, almost big enough

to hide. These marks lasted longer
I bet than whatever JON+JO
had going on. Who's so sure

of themselves that they'd ignore
the signs, so sure they can't
get caught? Sofia + Phoebe

Akran + Josefina      Amy from 2013
with love. By then I had a thousand
seasons of practice, kissing my palm

and squinting. Where the weather agrees
the bamboo will grow an inch
every hour, you read from a plaque.

Yesterday in the grocery store
I polished an eyelash from your glasses
and proposed while your arms were full

with what would be our third meal
together, the angel hair noodles
and parmesan and the red

onions and 3$ wine and zaftig tomatoes
with extra virgin olive oil and oranges
for the morning and aloe vera-based lube

and the celery      the eggs      the dark
chocolate      the spinach      the thyme
the you and me    L+Q   J+N   G+A

who also burned their garlic bread,
F who wouldn't have met if D
4 ever hadn't slept late, S+Z

nervous to remember
what they wanted
to be the early days.

You run a hand over these names
carved like nails down the back
of the bamboo, still growing

despite those vandals, emerald
branches a little day-drunk
off the Santa Anas but poised

as they lift the love notes up
to the spring clouds. You're looking
at me. You're taking out a blade.

**The lilies!**

Yes I bought them outside of any wedding   or Christian funeral
   and I walked home lopsided from the corner store
with no woman's routine to fulfill
      but my own desire
           the lilies nodding against my shoulder
In the kitchen I pull the whittler's knife
    from my head   the one that always asks
         what more you can give  up
     I take the old blade
cut the paper and rubber bands that corset the lilies   trim their long stems
   at a slant under running water   until each lily stands tip-toe
       in its own cup   bowl   pitcher
set on any clear space around the apartment
          to tender the only calendar
                   I'll hear now
The days painted out
        by the tight buds   chrysalis-pale   beginning their slow blink open
    the lilies  the lilies   gone pink
  into somebody's clean laughing mouth        pink as good prosciutto   a curlicue
    of white fat fluting the magenta   red confetti pollen down the middle
      of these stargazers   their deep smell that swaddles the rooms
sinking a spring into pillows and curtains   even when the blooms fade
  to moth wings circled around the burning stamen
      The petals drop translucent to the marble table   the bookshelf   the floor
and a craving
   washes my chest again for these delicious facts        to wake and see lilies
    or her voice popping over the phone like espresso in the silver pot
or the way those green stems tangle under water in a glass vase like blankets
                blankets and legs
    Once a grasshopper finagled three flights
up to the bedroom window
   just to sip from the head of a flower on the black nightstand   the body enveloped
     in the sweet drink of it        the whole world  a lily
       and why deny this any longer–
    so big I could carry
       nothing else

# Resolution

> Time to us is sarcasm, a slick and treacherous monster with a jaw
> like a furnace incinerating every moment of our lives.
> —Abraham Joshua Heschel, *The Sabbath*

3 pm on a Tuesday & I'll bite the calendar if it looks at me
like that again / with its white squares like lace curtains
drawn tight over the windows of a house I'm not good
enough to live in    I keep misreading the metal signs to
BEWARE OF GOD I'm unaccomplished unwanted
unaware / unconscious unbelievable unbrushed
unforgivable understood    I'm made of blue light & split
ends / Guilt lines the soles of my shoes & I only know time
passes because I've clocked enough of it for groceries &
another bill's due    /    Every so-called morning I wake up
in my teenage bedroom with the same voids clawed over me
What's time with this hot air /    these open gutters of old
feeling /    to fall through    /    arbitrary as any american
holiday / These hours I am never more than an inch
from tears / Around me the walls have long arms but I'll cut
a red exit    /    I'll be cold stars & the clean snap of the second
hand calling forth a new year /    new me baby / when breath
comes easy as that mechanical twitch onward / I want a year
that looks good naked a year with no murder when the new
facts I learn about other people are not terrible / A year
bigger than another date in the electronic checkbook of our
many employers    /    What's time with all these sad dreams
in the way /    Through the financial district I walked last
December / with more than the general sense of dread
watching    their office windows fracture the final sunset
of that alleged month / their buildings silvered & spiked
like failed spaceships as the fog bled into the rootless dark
of a new year    Now the president's voice emerges from every
surface & I'm thinking of the 3 weeks during the Paris
Commune    when they named the days for flowers
that a person could smell & touch & see grow
The tangerines here are drier each summer like a dead man's
lip /    & like a corpse    the weather slumps forward through

the calendar   /   Spring lightning in September & the sun
still noon-drunk all winter until it's never not fire season   I
don't want to be in the moment        The moment is trying
to kill us  /  I want the drag race momentum of a promise
I have so far kept  /  I'm counting down now to midnight on
this June Tuesday in the summer of my enemies        Like
the names of lost cats I call out my sins      & yes the others
I forgive for being as late & foolish      / Yes I too am slow
& regret more than what I do but inside regret is a white
bird whose long neck the oil companies have not yet wrung
A bird whose defense is duh   flight   /    & I'm running
through  /  the house to gather my wrongs where I left them
the ones congealed and crusted / the wine glasses ringed
with my mouth's peeled shadow /    the vases of funeral
flowers gone sepia / all the dirty mirrors uncovered    &
the sink is so full of lonely dishes I can hardly turn the faucet
but look how this tap water sparkles better than any
top shelf champagne   /    I'm toasting every car on the 101
everybody trapped in this particular rush hour / Let us be
better than our lost days    /    Let them blur into wet paint
All our wrongs I throw up into shards of fireworked glass
the whole porcelain cabinet of shame cracked to gunpowder
& I'm barefoot in the intersection open-mouth kissing
the air  /  like a goldfish with the world's longest memory
for a goldfish   /    the time coiled into flashing yellow guts
Now happy new year say it back   happy   happy   say it

## Libations

Kneeling on the bedroom floor I'm circled
by a thousand glasses full to the lips
with how I've taken birth control: hot mulled
cider, pineapple juice, Manischewitz,
the tap waters of various countries
cupped in my hands, sips from what the lovers
are having tonight, dregs of black tea leaves,
spinach smoothies, red slushies, whatever's
in reach around 9 to swallow the pills
easy and pink as a sunset. I've known
what I want but forgot where the shame is.
I'll take it with the dry salt of my own
spit if I must, head thrown back with a real
laugh like an orgasm, undeniable.

# Chanel No. 5

*After Melanie & Arabelle*

Nana, who would sing NAZI PIGS!
at whoever she saw exiting
the country club, kept her bottle by the sink.
You spritz it on your knees so it flies
around when you're dancing, she explained
to me, stooped on the formica counter
before she pinched my back so I sat up
straight. Her fingerprints still web the square vial,
the almost-invisible glass adorned
with the name of a woman who slept
through the Occupation in a Ritz suite
with a propaganda officer.
A woman who, there's no sexy way
to say it, made career ladders
out of fascism. This scent
Nana pressed unknown to her wrists,
her neck. The nights out in heels
like hi-hat cymbals, the days
waiting for no letters to hold, no news
from the cousins, entire fields of roses
crushed and drained in the air around her.
When she ate orange peels on the Sunset trolley
to her first job, the pins and needles
fizz of aldehydes when she eloped
in a dark blue negligée at the age
I am now, the same sillage
through the blacklisted years she walked
with her red nails curled to fists
in her pockets, thumbs on top
of her knuckles, ready.
Over her empty vinyl raincoat hangs
the musk like new names
picked for Hollywood.
The perfume's curdled, the amber
clotted down the sides. You'll love
it, she'd say. You've got to learn to swing.

**Walking through the husband**

Back to the archives I'll go slow in the same green
dress as last August, daring you to see
the alleys coming to me like sugar melted in hot lemon juice
thick as tears next to the falafel place I know
the deli will be crowded but I need someone to touch
my shoulder and move into the skein of streets
where the apartments are small enough to see
marbled clouds button up the sky
brushes off crumbs of sun on cobblestone below
a cello throbs along the Marais which I keep mispronouncing
like it means "husband" so that's what I'm walking through again
let desire wear down my good shoes here
all my theoretical husbands turning to frown
in their 3rd-story windows speaking that soft way
along bridges to the cathedral we cross
my heart you promised
you'd call if you ever found that earring and nobody called, nobody
sees me run from the fruit stand in the storm water
down this drink then eat on the sheets
of rain I'll say I'm not used to such bright air
out my wishes– if I peel this orange in one go
I'll be a nice girl, dreaming
what I'm supposed to
want silverware and anniversaries
in a clean line the orange could spiral
staircases leading to you & only
I was taught what any kiss needs
a future, it can't be left
unanswered, here I bite
to the seed and it's still
sweet. There is no other ending.

## Jewish Geography as According to Aunt L

Of course I know. Ask me anything. My home
planet dangles red off a branch
beyond the canopy. Crack it open
and each seed is the word
for sky and heaven both. Call my name
and half the women at the party turn around.
Turn the map facedown,
now it's a tablecloth. Here is a park bench
where your grandfather once had stopped
to double-knot his shoes. Here
is someone's most small cousin
spinning with her arms out,
pomegranate juice a sparkle on her face.
Through these countries of sudden noises
you will find anywhere
you go through the terribleness, dinner
and an argument and people
sneezing with their full bodies.
My home planet, you can fit in your pocket.
We move, we move, atoms rock back and forth
in place, in prayer, light after light becomes honey
on the skin. Where you touch, sweetness, wheels of fire.
The front door of the synagogue
laughs open. Next week, a wedding. Who's dead?

**shvarts-apl**

*Yiddish, rare; "black apple"; pupil of one's eye; beloved*

only fits in my mouth because we're looking
at each other        and the black of your eyes
swells      how you must've looked at the one tree
on the street outside the earliest house
you remember       the house you talk about
when you're tired and making bad jokes

a place I can hear even if it's not my rotten dream
fenced as a grudge        the lonely rooms
we're growing out of but never mind
those broken windows now        look at this tree   stretching
between us       while we kiss instead of check traffic
the fiddle string pull of the wood's own rising
is here      sweet as the someplace deep where roots go      sweet

as the shifting dark laced      through these criss cross limbs
braiding snowdrop blooms in the wind        in any sky
we're under        every leaf a parrot
green shimmy and there      on a high branch        red-
freckled   the first apple so far        lush
with its black opal seeds      wet & winking

**Horror movie finale with 5 things I can see,**
**4 things I feel, 3 things to hear, 2 scents, 1 taste**

It lurks, each time,
the knowledge
that when I turn
wet & naked
in the shower, the steam
will clear into
some lobsterific ghoul.
Yes, the moment
I lift my dripping
head from the faucet,
every chain text cryptid
and billionaire
on his 4th heart transplant
will be ready, hook-eyed,
to collect my organs.
Any movie poster
half-glanced,
any whisper
of a ghost
story and it's all
I can remember.
Quite sure I am
that while I,
tomato-soft,
wait
for the deep
conditioner to set,
a mutant python
pushes through
the pipes and
something else
with long legs
and a jaw to match
cracks down the hallway
to the bathroom where even
now a knife shreds
the shower curtain
for chocolate syrup
to hypno-swirl the drain

and when I turn
this time, there is
only more water.
And each time
the mirror
misfires, slips me
clean from my body
and I know
it's the last
time, I'll be
a haunt forever,
a gap where
the tooth was,
some prelude
to blood, when
someone's panting
in the reflection
but I'm
a thousand yards
gone— still
the mint green tile
rises beneath bare feet
as I watch
hands finger comb
a fog blurred
on the glass
these hands that press
in another ovation
and melt
the coconut oil
down legs
down the skin
that waits
each time I leave
and then find
a way back
to running blue.

## Overcast

No matter how you wash the sheets, the stains won't lift.
The baby blue you loved as a kid won't resurface
under this field of grays, the soft fossil of your body

preserved in the center. It's the color of a recurring
cough, or the sky downtown when the air's been tight
for days and you swear the smog will crack into rain,

staring as you wait outside the doctor's office,
or the color of water drawn from a well
where you've thrown the evidence of your life

during your life. What you could not hold
you made the well swallow, trusting the dark
to melt it down. Except you're thirsty now,

and the water you pull out froths in the bucket.
There's nothing else to do but drag the rest up
yourself from the deep shadow, the diaries

with their ink running, the rusted
silverware, the pregnancy tests so cheap
they come in 2-packs, a cell phone stuck

on the same jagged voicemail, the cigarettes
you smoked to stay awake floating on the slate
water. You've been drinking all that, these years

you pressed underground, you've rinsed your hair
with this silt and let it dry. Sometimes you wait
to catch your breath, covered in the same grime

as the playing cards and home videos,
the violin you quit. You keep going,
bringing out the bedposts in pieces,

toothbrushes, drained bottles of bleach and shampoo,
all the ways you tried to kill a dirt you could not see.
Each piece you raise from the brack, wipe clean enough

with the hem of your pink pajama shirt
and set it down on the new grass,
even the spider nest of hands locked

mid-caress, mid-choke, the many palm lines
splintered. You see the whole cacophony in the sun,
you can touch each thing to weigh the years

against what you know now, and maybe
the looking is a kind of bonfire, maybe an ash
settles and the water runs clear, there's clear

water on your face in the spinning
thresh of the old sheets and the silver
machine's dinging, the laundromat's

lit up like a spaceship, stars of rain
flashing by the blue windows, the air soaped
with the lavender daily worries of strangers

but you can leave now, leave your loose
change behind for the next fool,
empty your pockets and go.

I really think
that I don't mind
people sleeping
during my films,
because I know
that some
very good films
might prepare you
for sleeping
or falling asleep
or snoozing.
It's not to be
taken badly at all.

—Abbas Kiarostami,
*interview*

**#1**

Real as the mosaic wind between screen
and projector is the dream where my first
teeth slid like zippers along my gums, or
the world where boiled eggs charge cameras
so I'm running down market aisles for
"batteries" before the shoot, or me and
the host of my favorite documentary
shtupping in a haunted house. *Awful lot
of rain,* says my 8th grade crush, which I know
can't be true since our hometown is in flames
again. Arms rung with gilt, the aquanaut
troops in, fins backwards, from the Louvre, alarms
ringing, to sift the sea through gold frames and
wait. Swear that's how it happened, how it was.

*What?     Swear that's how it happened, how it was?*
*Your point of view? Your memory of wounds?*
The detective leans on the table, pocks
of old interrogations splayed under
her knuckles. *You'd wreck a man's life.* Suited
tremors pace behind the one-way glass. *Who*
*would believe you?* A bare light swings from this
scalped ceiling, and mirrored in the table's
skinned metal, your face, I recognize:   that
bus driver who took me home without fare,
the day they confirmed the judge and each sound
bite husked my bones. *My daughter has the same,*
you nodded at my blue beach cruiser. Street
lamps flare. *Think it's safe to ride past sunset?*

Lamps click off– it's safe to meet past sunset
or there wouldn't be so many of us
gossiping by candles in this kitchen.
These women are taller, and move how I
might, mothers of mothers of mothers back
to our first waters. Then the door fractures.
Angels of History tear them from sight.
I ask the last tante *Where are we?*     *Night of
Murdered Poets,* suggests the old book still
open on my desk. We melt to a chain,
strung across a meadow of painted film.
Your hands all in mine, we march through lilac
wreaths until you slip over the cliff's edge.
Lilies pulse, the umber rabid with breath.

## #4

Under lids that pulse with your rapid breath,
my best brown eyes trace storm clouds.     Soon you'll turn
and say I dropped the pasta, or maybe
wave from a cruise ship. Only one to see
my zit cream and dandelion bedhead,
to feel me snap like a blown umbrella.
I was shy as a driver in LA
rain, sleeping next to you in this pinwheel
body. What the doctor deems     *hypnic jerks*
     *as residual of early trauma,*
you call my puppy twitch. The night whistles
a slow dance, where the small forest of us
swoons above swept-off sheets. That apricot
heat balloons through my hours tomorrow.

**#5**

Heat blooms through my hours of sweat today
but I made my face waterproof. Weeping
figs cough outside the courthouse where my dress
stands modest as doubleknot laces, hair
tied like a left dog. By mistake, I walked
into the last trial naked. This time
I don't forget to bring the cut skull of
my child self for evidence, bruises wet
on our mouth. I forgot nothing. I feel
however cool I thought 18 would be when
I was 12. For a jury of someone
else's peers, I fold my posture to a
shape they might hear. The head spits and stares up
the street that arches its back to meet us.

## #6

Down the street, that arc of midnight beams up
from the church bells to my front yard. Somehow
it's still bright here, the sky like expired
film. This must be a kind of pollution–
exhaust and headlights that the poor clouds have
rendered from the daytime into white shmaltz.
I feel holy for not driving. There's no
stars but I can see jasmine, pink little
shrieks on the wrought-iron fence, a plum tree
that won't flower, green tulips in rows straight
as only a kid could plant. The gate waves
open and like always, just when I hope
my puppy stays put, he zips out, I chase
after him and the lightning haze swallows.

#7

The aftershocks shake like a swallow's hymn

when the livestream of my temple goes red

then static as smoke over the camps full

again the camps that were never empty

wire cages at the archives smother

every lost and stolen mirror bolted

like my nails to the hospital tile

while a blackberry rope pulls whatever

I thought was my woman body towards his

shadow under the burnt stage lights I lose

the lines to Hamlet so I start shouting

*FIRE* for the theatre of reparations

officers and flames wide as Hollywood

scream against the hollow door of my jaw.

*Seems as if the whole soul does fly from you*
*for such sights,*        says my uncle    the rabbi
as you dip rugelach in your tea. Dew
winks on the ivy at Chez Marianne.
        *I don't know how I should talk about it,*
I shrug at this man who squints just like me.
*Dreams sans inquiry are letters unread.*
*What do we learn out from this?*        You gesture
your black swan of a coat sleeve for answers.
*To sleep near a dictionary?        A dream*
*is to prophecy as heartbeat to waltz.*
*Who can choose when to dance?*        My uncle, gone
wars ago, checks his wristwatch, which returns
with him into the record of my blood.

**#9**

Wind hums into the wrinkles of my map,
crumpled until the corners of Paris
I remember best can touch: Notre Dame
rolls above Place des Vosges and every gate
holds June bouquets. Rosebush road now runs past
the memorials, past secondhand books,
past abalone buildings whose shutters
blink sly as cats, it stretches exactly
where we swung our feet over that silk scarf
of a river, the days I cupped your grin's
hot ember. You sail another last kiss
off the neon street below as lindens
burst through the balcony and in my bed
here, I brush yellow petals from my eyes.

## #10

There, brushed honey gold, spun from irises
to raw silk hems and a whale bone corset,
the bodice like whole oranges peeled for
a wish. A dress for the woman you want
to be, that handful of rosewater, lace
cut for an hourglass, a dress that laughs
with you, last thing you'd wear on a good day,
nightgown that draws your own mother-of-pearl,
just come in the mail. But it doesn't fit
me. However I twist, the lingerie
is empty. I've got a thousand-yard-stare
for a body, cracked watch face, sand, a skin
away from the bad times. Did I not grow
at all after what I won't think about—

## #11

All that I won't think about rings after
me like tin cans on some newlywed's car.
Before I leave the therapist's office
I'm gone, the same driftwood as a daytime
moon. Last night my bedroom flaked into crime
reports. That's what I saw. In the waiting
room, how the plastic toys flare on their gray
carpet, that's what kills me. I didn't think
I'd get past 18 either but again
into the street which is only a street
and that buzz which is, apparently, an
ambulance, I jump back without thought here,
a waterfall of reflex laughing, I
cross so I guess I didn't want to die.

**#12**

Where Sunset crosses Hope, the August fog
cartwheels through morning, now a discotheque
of traffic signals. No one else is up
yet. Earlier each year, star jasmine comes
to places you touched, in this world we both
live on. I think your name how a blue jay
smacks into a window and there you are,
tall as forever. The sidewalk riptides
until I remember where I am and
I'm running, I've got you, I'm doing it
I'm beating the absolute teeth from a
pedophile, with stop signs, with the brass
section, in my good raincoat. Say your side
of the story in this blinking green mist,

even with a blank gun I never miss.
I've got straightening irons and cheese knives,
harp strings, bullet-point pens, got a bat-mitzvah
-party's worth of low-heeled shoes, all nesting
in your chest. Me, shaking a piggy bank
from the top floor of the Empire State
Building and that's you, shot through with wishes
on the ground. Into breadcrumbs I tear you,
I make you the new tongue of a church bell.
Let a watermelon bloom from your gut,
let chandeliers crack, let champagne explode,
I wring your handprints from my heart as you
drop Challenger Deep, and in the tidal
wake of my unforgiving, I let go.

#14

I wake up in the garden, indigo
inside the shvarts-apl, the wet pupil
of a new moon. They're under my nightgown
first before feathering the rest of me—
blues from each bad word, blood dry where I was
held to flame, was left, was gone, secrets now
a cat's cradle of muscle to feel what
I could not then. The street in front becomes
a river, and the flashing sound pulls all
the neighbors out in their own pajamas
and batterings as we make our ways down
through the ephemerals grown from the last
fire, and find the water cool on our hands
real as any mosaic breath between        sleep.

# #15

**(nightmare theory)**

oh    this reeling mosaic,[1] wind beneath sleep.
aftershocks shake you like a swallow's hymn.[7]
harp strings, pens, bullets,[13] don't know what you need
from the bad dream's meadow of painted film.[3]
night hums into the wrinkles of your mind,[9]
your points of view, your memories[2] loose chalk
in your mouth. you forget nothing,[5] you find
it under eyelids pulsing rapid[4] locked
as waterfalls of chemical reflex[11]
render daytime to circuitry. white schmaltz[6]
clots through morning,[12] now flashback discotheques,
fear you know natural as heartbeat to waltz,[8]
the body like a whole[10] orchard's blessed roots,
a cat's cradle of neurons[14] to bring you through.

And I walk around
slowly, as though
I were carrying
a pitcher full
of questions
on my head.
I whisper them
in a low voice.
I am afraid
that they may
splash out
from my memory.

—Bella Chagall,
*Burning Lights*

## Habit

The dog's dead but I keep walking
        around the same time, nothing more than the days

to pull me and my blue coat
        through this neighborhood where you can talk

to yourself without anybody noticing,
        where the weeping fig trees curl over the long gray

line of the sidewalk so that from where I am,
        the path goes forever, like one of those drawings

where they teach you how to fake
        perspective. I know I'm older when I stop wanting

to strangle the girl I was and try to hold her instead.
        For years I trusted my bones, the way my left big toe crossed

under the others as a lucky charm
        and then the doctor said he'd never seen

such advanced bunions. Now there's a knot worn
        into half my shoes as though the leather can still breathe by itself.

Now apply that formula to the mind: a key
        rubbed smooth so it can fit any gate marked HAZARD,

or roots clawing for better earth, more air
        until the whole street splits. Gd but I'm tired, tripping

over what I already know. The traffic noise
　　　　makes you think you're moving faster than you are, a snail

who feels every inch of street and recognizes
　　　　only the grain of yesterday's trail. One summer Wilshire

became a film strip. Every other time I'd walked
　　　　down the boulevard burnt sugar-thin, exposed again,

each step then echoed inside the frame,
　　　　inside all the other steps, the old moods pale

and ringing cataracts. Around me the past's edges
　　　　blurred silver and I left the country for someplace

I hadn't been sad before. They say
　　　　how you spend your days is how you spend

your life so most people I know are a bad week
　　　　from destitution and everybody needs the same epiphany

three times before it sticks. I'm growing
　　　　my hair out in case I have to burn it off. I lose

count of the part-time jobs, therapists, and men
　　　　I've had, and I can't remember when I started

doing this but if there's a plant straggled down
　　　　on the sidewalk here, some muddy plumeria,

some jacaranda bloom creased as a sleeve
        somebody's sobbed into, I'll pick them up,

the crushed plants. I put them over my chest
        in the deep pocket of my grandfather's blue coat,

a man I know through this worn shape,
        our loose shoulders, these brass buttons that shine

where he pressed his fingers each morning,
        the tiny hole from a lost union pin, the pocket thumping

with wishbone twigs and cactus leaves,
        hopeful as salamander tails, thumping until I'm home

to put them in a cup by a window
        so they can be graceful a little longer. There's the myth

of lizards growing back whole from one cut
        wriggling limb, and another one about hearts. You don't have to believe me

but I swear the orange marks that dust this coat,
        they must be colors from my grandfather's first city job,

painting backdrops for the movies. This orange
        dropped from a horizon built stroke by stroke under his young

and sure hand, the paint swelling
        into a carnival, or a palace balcony. No, tear it down,

let's give them the whole sky, all the people gathered
        before the canvas, everybody gone. Let it be a high sun with clouds

soaking up the shades like perfume in air
        for the big scene where there's only gentle reasons to cry

from here on and they're dancing as though
        the crowd's never moved another way, the gestures

that labor to the whole: their muscles pulling clean
        through memory to a twirl, the breathing that lifts

the notes of the song, stitches in the costumes,
        technicolor film spun frame by frame into the camera

and behind it all, the patient brushstrokes
        of the sun undeniable, so bright you could set a truth to it

even as night steeps where I am, back
        at the house inside another bad year, and before I turn

on the lamp, I find a glass for this splintered leaf
        of a ghost plant, I guide the fragment in like a baby to a warm bath

in the last murmur of dusk and rinse out the coffee mug
        and fill it with cold water and after I sprinkle my lost and found flowers

my votives my toasts and I didn't realize how many
        there are here, how full, and I drink from the same cup.

## Perennial

Blood down the gray shower drain
like color sunk from a sunset.

When the landline shook
with his hot breath behind it

I stayed barefoot in the front yard soft
from a winter rain, lifting bags of tulip bulbs

not thinking a damn thing,
not me or my hands or the dirt.

Now the flowers are umbrellas
opening from the crowded station

of the ground. Between myself
and the arms of a man I hate

is a length of time, green, thin
as matchsticks, breakable, sending

out roots. I climb from the calendar
with orange & yellow mouths.

**Persimmon season**

It was growing the whole summer,
between the green persimmons out front
which melt in with their own round leaves,
the fruit invisible until they're too bright to look
away. Our days slow with sex,
the thick yellow curtains always drawn
against the heat so that light falls
through the color washing the bedroom
in a gold you could swim through, honey
spilling under the door as if every hour
was that time just before sunset, when each corner
of the apartment holds the wet glint
of another toast. The hours you practiced
the same nocturne on the piano, the same phrase
drawn note by note, your fingers careful
down the contours of the song. The hours I gathered
last week's pink and white lilies, rinsed the vases
and filled them with new water and pennies, cut
the stems at a slant to make the blooms last
another few days. In September
when I come back from the train station
without you, I find the street flamed
with persimmons, orange lanterns hung
from every branch lighting a way on if not home
and a bite of this, the stolen fruit,
skin tight at the first chill,
the cinnamon-heavy flesh, your torso
and the long shadows again.

## I say I'm engaged, actually


so as much as I'd love to get
drinks or your number or followed home
I'm already taken! I explain smiling
as I waggle my left hand to sparkle
the glass ring I bought at the flea market
for this exact purpose.
It's true though, I am engaged
by gravity as experienced
bicycling downhill, by eavesdropping,
a fresh latke with sour cream and chives
and hot little pecks of red pepper flakes, and how I pant
catching the yucca's whisper up the street proves
that I am spoken for

## Engram

Oh we go out as much as possible but memory
really walks me. If I have to cash a check, memory

wants to go through dumpsters.
When I play fetch, memory

brings back broken plates. Won't learn
any tricks, not a twirl for my memory.

I tie the rope to my wrist but it's no matter
I've got to follow the zigzag tether of memory

through town, whistling myself numb
for dates and times only to find memory

running down the middle of the road.
This whole neighborhood howls if memory

whimpers. The sharp parts are still teething,
the furniture scrawled from memory

scratching the door until I make room.
Memory, stay close to me. Memory,

heel. Memory, go sprawl on somebody's lawn,
trace the rosemary bushes for animal spirits

thrumming blue stars, watch the breath
that shivers blades of grass and

I'll be on the street corner cooing
come on girl          come on

## Prayer to be said at a graveside

By contrast, Eastern European tkhines were...published in little booklets addressing one or two topics, usually on inexpensive paper with small, difficult-to-read type.

-Chava Weissler, *Voices of the Matriarchs*

*For Racelle Rossett*

give us    these books   for a few centuries made from
good luck in    scraps   how the women simmered
all    the bones and peels to
our    mouthfuls of golden broth  the whole tkhines
deeds    prayers for winter hunger
and may    blooming in yiddish to be read aloud
our feet    rocking until the good brides could breathe
not stumble    through the verses from memory of the pages
in this world    ruffled as the bird's wing of a scar
and    across a stomach   they who bound g-d to promises:

may we    unlock wombs   bear smart babies   make evil eye
sit    like a good wolf   catch sunset
at rest    in a wick's flame   printed
in the    mother tongue   paper cut for the
next world with    daily shapes of a woman's life   their
saintly    hands apple-firm over their eyes   the pamphlets
   largely were written by

women those    anonymous authors   like candles
who    grow with each layer of beeswax   they
have been    gathered   the words  the fragments
buried    through time in their minds
and now    you hardly see the earth   you walk through
dwell with    the unknown
the holy    great-great-grandmothers   a
divine presence    humming still in your blood

*The title & left hand text comes from* Seyder Tkhines, *translated & edited by Devra Kay.*

**Fire sale**

I'm saying there will be no history but
I bought last year's defunct datebooks / cheaper
for notes I must believe I could use / each page
an empty place setting / On this table I cough
my own verse I WANT NOTHING I NEED
NOTHING and that's not true / I planned breakfast
for us / In this country of sudden noises
my grandparents got married after three weeks
of knowing each other so right now instead
of the next fascist I throw rice through the air / bury
daffodils in the crying ground with no shovel
but my animal hands / I'm soaking stale challah
in cinnamon milk and eggs for tomorrow
and is my arm not sore from vaccinations against
a few possible deaths? / Won't this night cream
save my skin for the future? / When dawn comes with
another body count and drags our shadows
to the kitchen floor / doesn't that make us
sundials? I have the lullabies for children
I do not

## View from magic hour

It's that time when the city behaves
like an orange peel, squeezing gold
from every pore as the sun hits just
so: those stucco apartment walls softer
than the lips of magnolia petals
underneath the nests that starlings
must've crafted from lost jewelry, tucked up
on the shoulders of saints by the church door,
their stone faces weathered away until
they're girls again, and the people here too,
squinting in this honeycomb cloud
at the Crossroads of the World as if
everybody stepping off the Sunset
Rapid can see their best love anywhere
they look, by windows, on wings, in the broken
sidewalks, and in those very cracks, the same light
pulls wild clover from the hidden dirt
for the bees, swirling low, and who knows where
among the skyscrapers that hive is
but there they go anyway, collecting
their public, secret joy.

*As for me in Los Angeles, I mostly saw walls*          begins
the winding creek of Varda's voice over her restored
film, about as long as a sleep cycle. *Murals as living,*
*breathing, seething walls,*          living in the sense
that they can be destroyed. *But these walls don't sell you*
*anything*          as she pans through Hollywood,
catching what anyone might see as they wait on a curb
for the light to change– the anonymous thrash
of traffic, billboards stilted in the public air, cut-out lips
and nails radioactively large and red in their frames,
or sometimes the ad takes extra scaffolding against
the sky, the pose reached outside its rectangle as though
the Lumière train really did crash through the movie
screen to offer the screaming crowd a Dr. Pepper. Same
as now, any flat space was marked with the best tricks–
technicolor, airbrush, sex, chiaroscuro, all-caps, jerking
the eye no worse than a toddler on a leash down
the street, demanding to look, remember, purchase.
A mural has a different song. A mural in the city feels
like a tree just glowing with limas from a block away,
the branches baby yellow and drooped over a private
fence, yours to pocket. Which also feels like a friend
waving from the other end of a subway station. *A face*
*suddenly in close-up with a persistent gaze.*          The first
mural of the documentary is not an argument for soda
or an accident but it does call your attention.
The Old Woman of the Freeway stares over the 101
and its dry ivy which believes it lives in a windstorm.
She is painted to the scale of memory on the side
of a hotel. Her hands are an olive tree. There's the lunar
halo of her hair, a few gray strands curling away,
then a blue moon pinned behind her, a cyanotype
thumbprint on the black space behind her, the same
thick dark as when you squeeze your eyes shut
trying to remember something important. Around her
brown nutmeg housecoat she holds a blanket
that the painter's real granny made, though the woman
here is an actress. The colors of the granny squares spiral
into each other, lavender ruby aquamarine ochre, yarn
like the layers of tags, *mythic serpent of signatures*
down a long wall where the opening credits flashed.

Lined with bricks and skin, she's got that expression of living in the desert all spring. The sky was open when she walked through the hills, only watching birds, leaves, healthy clouds, other people, no poreless grins or logos larger than her body. Now she's back to the city and realizing how much quiet space she could move within, just her   hands at rest and a blanket and whatever else the night held, all of this whitewashed a few years after the movie was shot and replaced with YOUR AD HERE. And it's impossible but I swear from shotgun I've seen those eyes driving home, floating bold through the smog.

## Hickey

You do love them, kisses you can carry
with you, a string of dark river pearls kept
warm under your collar, your mouth dizzy
just looking at that summer storm violet
over your chest, the red velvet clouds near
crackling. You love the shy ritual
after, a long turtleneck to cover
up those ruffled leaves of purple basil
that blush for me and all of our mornings,
worn soft– how your old blue shirt's frayed to lace
so when I wear it, with my legs swinging
off the counter as you futz with tea leaves,
you see plums, the plums that grow on my skin
backwards: petals, wind, to your breath again.

## Song written in your leftover hair

Every time, my Gd, like
I've been delicately
mauled by a werewolf
like there's a telephone cord
wrapped around my arm
down the lengths
of my legs, typewriter ribbons
and tuxedo threads teased
into spirals until anyone can see
that I am your tipsy maypole
that every black apple stem
twisted while reciting
the alphabet to find
the name of your future
lover ended up
under my blouse
along with the alphabet
in ink and the bumblebee
stripes of your stubble
and all the licorice curlicues
on a topographic map
to mark just how deep
this ocean goes
Yes yes even when I wash
my own hair, I find
these muddy tomato sprouts
tangled on the shower wall,
cursive in a language
I am learning
again I sound out
the dark scrawl of your postcards *Wish*
*you were here     you were here*

Every time I find these cypress shadows
and what sticks to you when I leave? The same webs of sun?

## Love language

Any tenderness I know, you learned same as me,
by sounding the sharp words out until you
could hold them. We're still latchkey tomatoes,
dirty vines tangled as hair running over dry
earth, grown where we can, no trellis, no neat guide
for our wanderings but each other. This smooth
grammar of lip gloss and borrowed shirts,
heads wild out the car windows, screaming
inside a good song, stripping down to go
jump right through a riptide, that push and pull another
knowledge. When I'm deep in the waves I can
look at you treading these currents. Who else teaches you
manners? How to cartwheel, to say
no and mean it, but we can fall & fall & find
out. Oh best best friends, split this
pomegranate and an hour with me, call me when
quiet is too thick to cut, call me
rabid with gossip, call me when you get home.
Sweethearts, did you know friendship & freedom carry
the same root? Did you know that with water,
under enough sun, even the most scraggle-tooth
vegetable scrap can grow back again & again?
What a garden here, what a syntax,
xylem poised as a group chat, us scallions,
yellow-gold beets, melon radish, holy basil, us
zucchini blossoms teaching the ground to laugh.

**on the first day of the general strike**

we filled the streets like stitches in blankets
like sap in maple trees like breath in wind
like hammocks like a heart like paper plates
after we made the whole foods a kitchen
& split a country club into breakfast
tables, & some of us grabbed another
biscuit, some of us napped, some read romance
novels as the sun on our skin sugared
to memory so we would never settle
for workday fluorescents, & the kids aimed
themselves & rolled down a blood emerald hill
on the golf course, worlds turning around them
on the first day this dirt began to leach
the old poisons, dreaming what else it could be

**talking cure**

She aptly described this procedure, speaking seriously, as a 'talking cure', while she
referred to it jokingly as 'chimney-sweeping'.

—Josef Breur, *Studies on Hysteria*

| *sillage* | *thirst* |
|---|---|
| by accident or not | you carried the meat and roses home |
| somehow you dropped | through the day's heat stroke |
| the old favorite perfume | the groceries    all that |
| you needed | to live |
| hidden roots blooming | heavy in your arms |
| wherever you went | now you're panting fully-dressed |
| a clear secret held in | on the edge of |
| a glass mouth | your shower    cold stutters |
| the red words | rushing out   the shock |
| almost rubbed way | makes you notice |
| after these years | how warm your skin is |
| and the routine you made | alone hiding from the sun |
| in slow motion | it's been said |
| there's no saving it | even water has a memory |
| the glass cracked wide | those same sounds |
| acid and musk | pooling with your sweat |
| like tidal waves | become a sea    become ice |
| swelling the room | a freshet to clean a burn |
| with a name like Hungry or Desire | drawn from underground to |
| dew on neroli | a blood orange's damp sigh |
| conjured to a feeling | now some gd's eye of a cloud |
| which clots the air | becomes rain |
| the fragments | soft on that woman's forehead |
| crying light | when she left the fainting couch |
| scratching the walls | for a crowd outdoors last century |
| all the hours before   a fog | and your face is wet |
| and you can try to step around it | another drop in this spiral even |
| as you cough up | your body is mostly |
| the absolute heart | that same long river |
| but you know | crouched in your human way |
| the only way out | you know |
| barefoot as you are | only this will save you |
| through the broken field | your cupped hands to your lips |
| towards any open window | and back again |

## Parc Monceau, September

Now and then I must do things I know
I'm lousy at, such as oil paints
or believing in Gd.

It was so easy before I knew
I was bad, mixing all my colors
together, thanking the clouds
for the good health of whales.

Soon enough it'll come back
to me, swaying below *The Apparition,*
another angel stepping recklessly large
into the bedroom, the wings
licking the rooftop blue
as a kitchen fire, all the light
crystallized to rock candy
of black, white, cerulean,
the mirrors and candlesticks thrown
into some kind of relief.

Again I'm clawing through a dry canvas,
eyes tight for the best answer
on how I'm supposed to see things.

Today at the park
as I was trying to catch
the sublime and et cetera
coming off a bridge built to look
older and more wise than it already is,
two very small girls asked to borrow my paints.

On my fanciest paper, big enough
to cover them both, the kids
sculpted out with their new hands the grass,
and then the sky,
with the rough of the page left blank
in the middle, plus a rainbow that goes
green red pink orange
purple, and the sun
gathered up in a corner.

And in the third place
between the lines of earth
and indigo, there's stick figures
floating with their own smiles, the fingerprints
of the artists still damp, so sure
in their vision that they gave me
the piece and ran off.

# Notes

The poem *Elsa la Rose (1966)* is inspired by Agnès Varda's documentary of the same name on Elsa Triolet and Louis Aragon, a pair of writers important to the French Surrealist and Communist movements.

Many of the initials in *Makeout Corner of the Botanical Garden* come from the Mildred E. Mathias Botanical Garden at UCLA.

*Chanel No. 5* follows the research of scholar Arabelle Sicardi, as well as the beauty rituals of women in my family.

"Shvarts-apl" was one of the favorite words of Yiddish poet Avrom Sutzkever. The line "the fiddle string pull of the wood's own rising" is inspired by his invented word "fidlroyz", meaning "fiddle-rose", a synesthetic union of beauty and sound.

*Manifesto in an unknown language, Top note,* and *Crush* all shared inspiration in Miranda July's 2020 film Kajillionaire, and I'm happy to have been part of that audience.

In *Dream Diary #3*, the phrase "Angels of History" comes from Walter Benjamin's 1940 essay "Theses on the Philosophy of History":

> *A Klee painting named Angelus Novus shows an angel looking as though he is about to move away from something he is fixedly contemplating. His eyes are staring, his mouth is open, his wings are spread. This is how one pictures the angel of history. His face is turned toward the past. Where we perceive a chain of events, he sees one single catastrophe which keeps piling wreckage upon wreckage and hurls it in front of his feet. The angel would like to stay, awaken the dead, and make whole what has been smashed. But a storm is blowing from Paradise; it has got caught in his wings with such violence that the angel can no longer close them. The storm irresistibly propels him into the future to which his back is turned, while the pile of debris before him grows skyward. This storm is what we call progress.*

The poem *Mur Murs (1981)* is inspired by Agnès Varda's documentary of the same name, and the mural *Old Woman of the Freeway* was first painted by Kent Twitchell in 1974. After it was erased in 1986 by a billboard company, Twitchell spent many years finding a new home for the mural before painting it on Los Angeles Valley College in 2016.

The poem *on the first day of the general strike* came together after listening to an interview with Sara Nelson, President of the Association of Flight Attendants-CWA, AFL-CIO.

In *talking cure*, the phrase "meat and roses" is inspired by the print *Cross Section of a Bouquet* by Nadezda Pliskova. The woman referred to in the line "soft on a woman's forehead" and in the epigraph is Bertha Pappenheim, called Anna O. in the writings of Josef Breur and Sigmund Freud. In her early twenties, she was treated by Breur, and the "free association" practice of modern psychology emerged from their sessions.

In *September, Parc Monceau*, the painting referenced in the third stanza is *L'Apparition* by Marc Chagall, 1918

I am very grateful to these publications and their editors for being homes for my poems before this book:

| *Engram* | Perpetual Doom Zine, Issue No. One: Navigation to Nowhere, 2021 |
| *Pith* | Dish Soap Quarterly, Issue 2, 2021 |
| *Top note* | Flaunt, September 2020 |
| *Jewish Geography as According to Aunt L* | CURA, Issue No. 20, Spring 2019 |

My endless thanks to Alyesha Wise and Matthew Cuban Hernandez for showing me how to live as a poet, and Dr. Barry Pohlman for making sure I knew how to take notes in high school.

I'm deeply grateful to the staff members of Stories Books & Cafe, Skylight Books, Junior High, and Da Poetry Lounge for fostering creative communities in Los Angeles over the years.

Thank you to Racelle Rossett for introducing me to the old tkhines, and keeping space for poetry and prayer in this world. Thank you to Dr. James Ragan for showing me Prague by foot, and making sure my line breaks are clean.

Thank you to the creative writing students of UCLA for being the best peers, and all of our incredible professors. Thank you Fred D'Aguiar and Reed Wilson for helping me get weird in workshop, and Harryette Mullen for guiding us through so many poetic forms. Thank you Anahid Nersessian for making the Romantics exactly as cool as they are, and for the only definition of "dialectics" I can consistently remember. Thank you Miriam Koral for introducing me to Avrom Sutzkever and so many more wonderful Yiddish artists. Thank you to my thesis advisor Daniel Snelson, for your evergreen advice and media recommendations.

Thank you Not A Cult and Daniel for letting me be late but making sure the book got done anyway. Cassidy Trier, thank you for bringing my poems to life with your incredible artwork. Julianna Sy, thank you for your utterly perfect formatting and attention to detail. A thousand thousand thanks for sam sax, I couldn't wish for a more brilliant and compassionate editor.

My best gratitude for my mom, who first showed me Agnès Varda movies, and my league of godparents. Thank you Aunt Penny and Uncle Gralin, and Aunt Lynda and Uncle Biff for helping me grow up.

One hundred glasses of champagne each to my first and best readers Nesha, Gen, Tamia, and Aneri, thank you for your sweet sweet notes and encouragement.

Thank you Benjamin and Skye for running around Paris.

Max and Arabelle, thank you for pulling me out to the desert to see the stars when this book was just a little idea for a zine called *I Hope This Chicken is Raw and We All Die*.

Veronika, thank you for being the best big sister a machshaifeh could ask for. Isabella, thank you for going through the grammar, and telling me when to just say it. Eden, thank you for jello shots and telling me which poems were best. Ariela, this book would not have been finished without your kitchen and all of our movie nights. Mehtab, thanks for the flowers.

# Index

Rhiannon McGavin has failed the driver's license test three times so far. She has performed from the Hollywood Bowl to the Library of Congress, as well as on NPR. Her work has been published by Tia Chucha Press, *Cura, Teen Vogue*, and *The Believer*. As a YoungArts Finalist in Spoken Word, she was nominated for the Presidential Scholar of the Arts. She is the 2019 recipient of the Fred and Edith Herman Memorial Prize from the Academy of American Poets. Rhiannon was the Youth Poet Laureate of Los Angeles in 2016. Her first poetry collection Branches is also available from Not a Cult. You can find her online and on the street, walking.

Published by Not a Cult, an imprint of Chapter House
Los Angeles, CA | Boston, MA
www.notacult.media


For information pertaining to distribution, rights, or permissions
please email books@notacult.media